Media Relations Mega Mastermind

Ashley Wiley-Morris Paretto

Copyright © 2023 by Ashley Wiley-Morris Paretto

All rights reserved.

No portion of this book may be reproduced in any form without written permission from the publisher or author, except as permitted by U.S. copyright law.

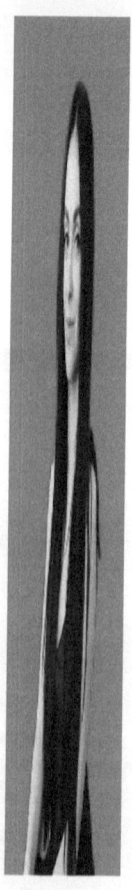

Chapter 1

Media Relations Mega Mastermind

What is the definition of media relations?

Media relations is the practice of building and maintaining relationships between an organization or individual and various media outlets. The aim is to establish a positive and mutually beneficial connection that can help disseminate information to a larger audience.

The media outlets could be traditional print and broadcast media such as newspapers, magazines, radio, and television, or digital media such as blogs, social media platforms, podcasts, and online news sources. The media relations professional is responsible for reaching out to these outlets and developing relationships with journalists, editors, and producers who can help promote their client's message.

The main goal of media relations is to generate positive media coverage that can help build awareness and credibility for a brand, product, or individual. This can be achieved through various tactics such as press releases, media pitches, interviews, and other forms of media outreach.

One essential aspect of media relations is understanding the various types of media outlets and their audience. Traditional media outlets such as newspapers and television networks have a broad reach and can reach a wide audience. However, they also have specific beats or topics they cover, and journalists have their preferred style of reporting. On the other hand, digital media outlets have more niche audiences and can be more targeted, but the competition for attention is fierce.

To be effective, media relations professionals must have a solid understanding of their client's audience and how to tailor their message to the appropriate media outlet. For example, if a company is launching a new product, a press release may be sent to trade publications or industry-specific blogs. However, if the product has a broader appeal, a media pitch to a local or national news outlet may be more appropriate.

The key to successful media relations is building strong relationships with journalists and editors. This involves understanding their needs, deadlines, and preferences, and providing them with relevant and timely information. Media relations professionals must also be able to respond quickly and effectively to media inquiries and be prepared to provide accurate and concise information to journalists.

In addition to generating positive media coverage, media relations can also be valuable in crisis management situations. When a company or individual is facing negative publicity, media relations professionals can help control the narrative and provide accurate and timely information to the media.

To be successful in media relations, it is essential to have a well-defined strategy that includes measurable goals and objectives. The strategy should be flexible enough to adapt to changing media trends and opportunities, and include a clear plan for reaching out to the appropriate media outlets.

In summary, media relations is the practice of building and maintaining relationships between an organization or individual and various media outlets. It is an essential component of any communications strategy and can help generate positive media coverage, build credibility and awareness, and manage crisis situations. To be successful, media relations professionals must have a solid understanding of their client's audience, build strong relationships with journalists and editors, and have a well-defined strategy that includes measurable goals and objectives.

- Why is building relationships with media outlets important?

Building relationships with media outlets is crucial for any organization or individual seeking to gain exposure and positive coverage in the media. As a media relations professional, I believe that cultivating strong relationships with journalists, reporters, and editors is one of the most important aspects of my job.

Firstly, having strong relationships with media outlets increases the likelihood of coverage. Journalists are constantly inundated with pitches, press releases, and story ideas, and they often rely on personal connections to decide which stories to pursue. If a journalist knows and trusts a media relations professional, they are more likely to give their pitch or story idea serious consideration. For example, if a tech company has a product launch coming up, and their media relations team has established relationships with tech reporters at various outlets, they may have a better chance of securing coverage for the launch.

Secondly, building relationships with media outlets helps to shape the narrative around an organization or individual. If a media relations professional has established a rapport with a reporter or editor, they may be able to provide background information or context that helps to shape the direction of a story. For example, if a company is facing negative press, but they have a strong relationship with a reporter at a major news outlet, the reporter may be more likely to present the company's side of the story in a fair and balanced way.

Thirdly, strong relationships with media outlets can help to establish an organization or individual as a trusted source of information. If a media relations professional has built trust with journalists and reporters, they may be more likely to turn to that organization or individual as a source for future stories. This can lead to more positive coverage and increased exposure. For example, if a financial advisor has developed a relationship with a personal finance reporter at a major newspaper, that reporter may turn to the advisor for quotes and insights on future stories.

There are many ways to build relationships with media outlets. One of the most important is to always be responsive and timely. Journalists work on tight deadlines and need quick responses to their inquiries. A media relations professional who is consistently responsive and helpful will build trust with journalists and increase the likelihood of future coverage.

Another key strategy is to be proactive in pitching story ideas and providing background information. A media relations professional who can provide journalists with interesting and timely story ideas is likely to build a strong relationship with that journalist. Additionally, providing background information or data that helps to shape a story can also be helpful in building relationships.

Attending industry events and networking with journalists in person is another important way to build relationships. This allows media relations professionals to put faces to names and establish a more personal connection with journalists. It also provides an opportunity to learn about the journalist's interests and preferences, which can be helpful in tailoring future pitches and story ideas.

In summary, building relationships with media outlets is essential for anyone seeking positive media coverage. By cultivating strong relationships with journalists, reporters, and editors, media relations professionals can increase the likelihood of coverage, shape the narrative around their organization or individual, and establish themselves as trusted sources of information. By being responsive, proactive, and building personal connections with journalists, media relations professionals can build long-term relationships that lead to positive outcomes.

- What distinguishes media relations from public relations?

Media relations and public relations are terms that are often used interchangeably, but they refer to distinct practices. Although they are related, there are some key differences between the two. In this chapter, we will examine what distinguishes media relations from public relations.

Public relations is a broad field that involves managing the relationship between an organization and the public. It encompasses a wide range of activities, including media relations, community relations, crisis communication, investor relations, and more. The goal of public relations is to promote a positive image of the organization and maintain a favorable relationship with stakeholders.

Media relations, on the other hand, is a subset of public relations that focuses specifically on managing the relationship between an organization and the media. It involves building relationships with journalists, editors, and other media professionals to promote the organization's message and manage its reputation in the media.

One of the key differences between media relations and public relations is the target audience. In public relations, the target audience is the general public, while in media relations, the target audience is the media. Media relations professionals work to build relationships with journalists, editors, and other media professionals to ensure that they have access to accurate information about the organization and its activities. This enables them to shape the narrative about the organization in the media.

Another difference between media relations and public relations is the way in which they are executed. Public relations activities can take a variety of forms, including press releases, events, sponsorships, and more. Media relations, on the other hand, is primarily focused on building relationships with journalists and securing media coverage for the organization. This can involve pitching story ideas to journalists, arranging interviews with executives, and providing background information on the organization and its activities.

Media relations professionals must also have a deep understanding of the media landscape. They must be familiar with the various types of media outlets, including print, broadcast, and digital, and understand the nuances of each. For example, pitching a story idea to a print newspaper requires a different approach than pitching the same idea to a television news program.

In addition to understanding the media landscape, media relations professionals must also be able to adapt to changes in the media industry. With the rise of social media and the decline of traditional media outlets, the media landscape is constantly evolving. Media relations professionals must be able to stay up-to-date on these changes and adapt their strategies accordingly.

One example of how media relations differs from public relations can be seen in the way that crisis communication is handled. In a crisis situation, such as a product recall or a data breach, public relations professionals must manage the organization's response and communicate with stakeholders. Media relations professionals, on the other hand, must work to manage the organization's reputation in the media. This can involve providing journalists with accurate information about the situation, addressing any misinformation that may be circulating in the media, and working to ensure that the organization's message is accurately portrayed in the media.

Overall, while media relations is a subset of public relations, it involves a distinct set of skills and activities. Media relations professionals must have a deep understanding of the media landscape, be able to build relationships with journalists and other media professionals, and be able to adapt to changes in the media industry. By working closely with the media, media relations professionals can help shape the narrative about an organization and ensure that its message is accurately portrayed in the media.

- What are the various categories of media outlets?

As a media relations professional, one of the most critical components of building relationships with journalists and securing media coverage for clients is understanding the various types of media outlets that exist. These outlets can differ significantly in terms of their audience, format, and editorial style, so it is essential to have a comprehensive understanding of their unique characteristics to tailor pitches effectively.

Print media outlets include newspapers and magazines, both of which can be either national or local in scope. National newspapers such as The New York Times or The Wall Street Journal are generally considered to be the most prestigious outlets and carry a great deal of weight in terms of influencing public opinion. Local newspapers, on the other hand, are typically smaller in circulation but are often more accessible for pitching local stories or events.

Magazines can vary widely in terms of their audience, ranging from niche publications to more general-interest titles.

Broadcast media includes television and radio outlets, which are often divided into national and local categories. National television news programs such as CBS Evening News or NBC Nightly News are considered to be top-tier outlets and can offer tremendous exposure for clients. Local television news programs can be more accessible to pitch and offer a way to target specific regions or markets. Radio stations can vary widely in terms of their audience, format, and geographic reach, so it is important to research each outlet to determine whether it is a good fit for a particular client or story.

Online media includes a broad range of outlets, from traditional news websites to social media platforms. Online news sites such as CNN.com or Politico.com are increasingly important outlets for media relations professionals to target, as more and more people are turning to the internet for news and information. Social media platforms such as Twitter or LinkedIn can also be valuable tools for building relationships with journalists and promoting client content.

Blogs and online forums are additional categories of media outlets that are becoming increasingly important in the media landscape. Blogs can be highly targeted to specific audiences and can offer an opportunity to reach niche communities or interest groups. However, it is important to be selective about which blogs to target, as not all blogs are created equal in terms of their credibility or influence.

Trade publications are another category of media outlet that are important to consider, particularly for B2B clients. These publications are often highly specialized and can offer an opportunity to reach specific industries or professional communities. For example, a company that sells medical equipment might target publications such as Medical Device and Diagnostic Industry or Healthcare Purchasing News.

Ultimately, understanding the various categories of media outlets is just the first step in developing an effective media relations strategy. Once you have identified the outlets that are most relevant to your client or story, it is essential to research each outlet in more depth to understand its editorial focus, target audience, and preferred pitching methods. For example, some outlets might prefer to receive pitches via email, while others might prefer phone calls or even social media messages.

In summary, the various categories of media outlets include print, broadcast, online, blogs and online forums, and trade publications. Each type of outlet has its own unique characteristics and target audience, so it is essential to research each outlet thoroughly to determine whether it is a good fit for a particular client or story. Once you have identified the outlets that are most relevant, it is important to tailor pitches to each outlet's preferences and editorial focus to maximize the chances of securing media coverage.

- How can one determine the appropriate media outlets to target their intended audience?

Determining the appropriate media outlets to target an intended audience is crucial for any media relations strategy. A media relations professional must have a deep understanding of their client's target audience and the type of media outlets that resonate with them. Here are some ways to determine the appropriate media outlets to target:

Conduct Audience Research:

1. The first step in determining the appropriate media outlets to target is to conduct audience research. This includes identifying the demographics, interests, and behaviors of the target audience. A media relations professional can gather this information through surveys, focus groups, or market research reports.

For instance, if a client is launching a new sports product, it's essential to target sports enthusiasts. This could involve researching which sports are popular in a particular region or age group, as well as analyzing the sports media outlets that the target audience consumes.

Identify Relevant Media Outlets:

1. After gathering information about the target audience, the next step is to identify relevant media outlets. A media relations professional should research and compile a list of media outlets that reach the target audience. This could include newspapers, magazines, TV and radio shows, blogs, podcasts, and social media channels.

For example, if the target audience for a product is young adults, it's essential to consider social media channels like Instagram and Twitter, which are popular among this demographic. On the other hand, if the target audience is older adults, traditional media outlets like newspapers and TV shows might be more effective.

Analyze Media Outlet Content:

1. Once relevant media outlets have been identified, it's essential to analyze the content they produce to ensure that it aligns with the client's message. Media outlets often have their own editorial stance and may only feature certain types of content.

A media relations professional should review the topics, tone, and angle of the media outlet's content to determine whether they are a good fit for the client's message. For instance, if a client is promoting a product that is environmentally friendly, it would be essential to identify media outlets that prioritize sustainability and green initiatives.

Determine the Right Format:

1. Media outlets use different formats to present information, and it's crucial to determine the appropriate format for the client's message. For example, if the client has a compelling story, it might be appropriate to pitch it to a newspaper or magazine for a feature article. On the other hand, if the client has a product launch, a TV or radio show might be more appropriate for a live interview.

A media relations professional should identify the media outlets that use the appropriate format for the client's message. This might involve researching the different types of content that media outlets produce, such as news articles, features, interviews, and reviews.

Utilize Media Databases:

1. Media databases are a valuable tool for identifying relevant media outlets and journalists. These databases provide contact information, editorial calendars, and insight into the type of content that media outlets produce.

A media relations professional can use media databases to search for media outlets that cover specific topics, as well as journalists who specialize in particular areas. This can help to streamline the outreach process and ensure that pitches are directed to the right people.

In conclusion, determining the appropriate media outlets to target an intended audience requires careful research and analysis. A media relations professional must understand the target audience, identify relevant media outlets, analyze the content of those outlets, determine the appropriate format, and utilize media databases to streamline outreach efforts. By following these steps, a media relations professional can develop an effective media relations strategy that reaches the target audience and achieves the client's objectives.

- What are the essential components of an effective media relations strategy?

An effective media relations strategy is an essential component for businesses and organizations that seek to establish a positive public image and foster good relationships with the media. It is the process of building and maintaining positive relationships between a business or organization and the media, which includes journalists, reporters, and editors. The primary goal of media relations is to promote a business or organization's message and to ensure that it is accurately and positively portrayed in the media. Here are some of the essential components of an effective media relations strategy:

1. Understanding the media landscape: To develop a successful media relations strategy, it is essential to have a good understanding of the media landscape. This includes knowing the different types of media outlets, such as print, broadcast, and online media, and the various platforms, including social media, blogs, and podcasts. It is also important to know the journalists, reporters, and editors who cover your industry or business and to be aware of the types of stories they typically cover.

2. Building relationships with journalists: One of the most important components of a media relations strategy is building relationships with journalists. This involves engaging with journalists regularly and providing them with relevant and timely information about your

business or organization. For example, a media relations professional could provide journalists with press releases, media advisories, and other materials that highlight a business or organization's key messages and initiatives.

3. Creating a compelling story: A compelling story is crucial to generating interest and coverage from the media. A media relations professional must be able to craft a narrative that is engaging and relevant to the media outlets they are targeting. This could involve developing a strong pitch, identifying key angles, and highlighting the unique aspects of a business or organization's story.

4. Understanding the news cycle: Timing is everything in media relations, and it is essential to understand the news cycle and how it affects the media's coverage. This involves keeping up to date with the latest news and trends in your industry or business and identifying opportunities to piggyback on news events or trends.

5. Preparing for media interviews: A key component of media relations is preparing for

media interviews. This involves identifying potential questions, practicing responses, and developing key messaging that aligns with a business or organization's brand and values. It is also essential to understand the media outlet's audience and tailor messaging accordingly.

6. Measuring success: Measuring the success of a media relations strategy is essential to determining its effectiveness and making improvements. This involves tracking media coverage, monitoring social media engagement, and analyzing metrics such as website traffic and sales figures.

Overall, an effective media relations strategy involves a combination of relationship building, storytelling, timing, and measurement. By understanding the media landscape, building strong relationships with journalists, crafting compelling stories, keeping up with the news cycle, preparing for media interviews, and measuring success, businesses and organizations can effectively promote their message and establish a positive public image.

- What is the process for creating a media contact list?

One of the essential components of a successful media relations strategy is developing a comprehensive media contact list. A media contact list is a database of media outlets, journalists, and editors who cover the topics and issues relevant to an organization's objectives. Creating a media contact list can be a time-consuming and daunting task, but it is essential for achieving media coverage and building relationships with key members of the media.

The process for creating a media contact list involves several steps, including researching media outlets, identifying key contacts, and organizing the information in a structured database. Below is a detailed guide on each of these steps.

Step 1: Research Media Outlets

The first step in creating a media contact list is to research the media outlets that are most likely to cover the organization's industry, products, or services. This can be done by conducting a search on Google, using media monitoring tools, or consulting industry directories.

It's important to research a wide range of media outlets, including local, regional, national, and international publications, as well as online news sites, blogs, and social media platforms. When researching media outlets, consider the following:

- Type of media outlet: Is it a print, broadcast, or online outlet?
- Audience demographics: Who is the target audience of the media outlet?
- Editorial focus: What are the topics and issues that the media outlet covers?
- Geographic reach: What is the coverage area of the media outlet?

Step 2: Identify Key Contacts

Once you have identified the relevant media outlets, the next step is to identify the key contacts within each outlet. Key contacts are the journalists, editors, or producers who cover the topics and issues that are relevant to the organization's objectives.

To identify key contacts, consider the following:

- Beat: What is the area of expertise of the journalist? Does their beat align with the organization's objectives?

- Recent coverage: Has the journalist recently covered topics or issues that are relevant to the organization?
- Contact information: Is the journalist's contact information available on the media outlet's website or social media platforms?

It's important to note that key contacts may change over time. Journalists may switch beats or move to different media outlets, so it's essential to update the media contact list regularly to ensure that it remains current.

Step 3: Organize the Information

After identifying the relevant media outlets and key contacts, the next step is to organize the information in a structured database. The database should include the following information:

- Media outlet name
- Type of media outlet
- Audience demographics
- Editorial focus
- Geographic reach
- Key contact name
- Key contact role (journalist, editor, producer)

- Key contact beat
- Key contact email address
- Key contact phone number
- Key contact social media handles

The database can be organized using a spreadsheet, such as Excel or Google Sheets. It's essential to keep the database up-to-date by adding new contacts and removing outdated information.

Examples:

Let's say an organization is in the healthcare industry and is looking to create a media contact list. The first step is to research relevant media outlets. They may start by searching on Google for healthcare news sites and find that Becker's Hospital Review and Healthcare IT News are two relevant media outlets.

Next, they identify the key contacts within each outlet. For Becker's Hospital Review, they find that Ayla Ellison is the managing editor and covers healthcare business and legal news. For Healthcare IT News, they find that Mike Miliard is the editor and covers healthcare technology news.

Finally, they organize the information in a structured database, as shown below:

Media Outlet	Type	Audience	Editorial Focus	Geographic Reach	Key Contact	Role	Beat	Email	Phone	Twitter Handle

- What is a press release, and how can one compose it?

A press release is a written statement that is typically issued by a company or organization to inform the media and the public about an event, product launch, achievement, or other newsworthy information. It is a valuable tool for getting media attention and generating coverage.

When composing a press release, it is important to keep in mind that journalists receive dozens if not hundreds of releases every day. Therefore, it is essential to make sure that your release is well-written, concise, and compelling to stand out from the crowd.

Here are the key elements of a press release and tips on how to compose each one:

1. Headline: The headline should be attention-grabbing and accurately reflect the content of the release. It should be brief, ideally no more

than 10-12 words. For example, "XYZ Company Launches Revolutionary New Product."

2. Subheadline: The subheadline should provide additional context or detail that supports the main headline. It can be longer than the headline but still brief, ideally no more than 20-25 words. For example, "The XYZ Widget Boosts Efficiency by 50%."

3. Introduction: The first paragraph of the release should provide a concise overview of the newsworthy information. It should answer the basic questions of who, what, where, when, and why. It should be no more than 2-3 sentences. For example, "Today, XYZ Company announced the launch of their new product, the XYZ Widget, which is designed to boost efficiency for businesses of all sizes."

4. Body: The body of the release should provide more detail and context about the newsworthy information. It should be organized in a logical and easy-to-read format, with paragraphs no longer than 3-4 sentences. It should include quotes from key executives or experts if

possible. For example, "The XYZ Widget is the result of months of research and development, and we are excited to bring it to the market," said John Doe, CEO of XYZ Company. "We believe that it will help businesses save time and money by streamlining their operations."

5. Boilerplate: The boilerplate is a brief paragraph at the end of the release that provides basic information about the company or organization, such as its history, mission, and products or services. It should be no more than 2-3 sentences. For example, "XYZ Company is a leading provider of innovative solutions for businesses, with a focus on efficiency, productivity, and customer satisfaction."

6. Contact Information: The release should include the contact information for a media relations or public relations representative who can answer questions or provide additional information. It should include the name, phone number, email address, and social media handles if applicable.

In addition to these key elements, here are some additional tips for composing a press release:

- Use clear, concise language and avoid jargon or technical terms that may be unfamiliar to the reader.
- Use active voice and avoid passive voice.
- Include relevant statistics or data to support the newsworthy information.
- Use bulleted lists or subheadings to break up the text and make it easier to read.
- Use quotes from experts or key executives to add credibility and interest to the release.
- Avoid excessive hype or exaggeration, as this can damage credibility and turn off journalists.
- Use proper spelling, grammar, and punctuation, and proofread carefully before sending.

In summary, a press release is a valuable tool for getting media attention and generating coverage. Composing a press release requires careful attention to detail, clear and concise language, and a focus on the newsworthy information. By following these tips and best practices, media relations professionals can increase the chances of their release being picked up and covered by journalists.

- When should a press release be issued?

As a media relations professional, knowing when to issue a press release is crucial for achieving optimal media coverage for your organization or client. A press release is an official statement distributed to the media to announce news or provide information about an event, product launch, or new development. It is essential to understand that a press release is not an advertisement; it is a news piece that must be newsworthy and relevant to the media outlet's audience.

The timing of a press release is key to its success. Timing can help to maximize media coverage, create interest, and generate buzz. Press releases should be issued when there is significant news to share, or when an organization wants to make a statement on a particular issue or development. However, it is important to avoid issuing too many press releases, as this can lead to media fatigue and ultimately reduce the impact of the news.

Here are some situations when issuing a press release would be appropriate:

1. New Product or Service Launch: Press releases can be issued to announce the launch of a new product or service. For example, if a company has developed a new mobile app, a press release could be issued to notify the media about the launch, its features, and benefits.
2. Promotions and Campaigns: Press releases can be issued to announce promotions, contests, or marketing campaigns. For instance, if a restaurant chain is running a special promotion for a holiday or special event, a press release could be issued to notify the media about the details of the promotion.
3. Company Milestones: Press releases can be used to celebrate company milestones, such as an anniversary or significant accomplishment. For example, if a nonprofit organization has reached a fundraising goal, a press release could be issued to share the news with the media and highlight the impact of the funds raised.
4. Mergers and Acquisitions: Press releases can be issued to announce mergers and acquisitions. When two companies merge or

one acquires another, a press release can be used to explain the details of the deal and what it means for the industry and customers.
5. Executive Changes: Press releases can be issued to announce executive changes, such as the appointment of a new CEO or executive director. This can help to provide clarity to stakeholders and the public about leadership changes and the direction of the organization.
6. Crisis Management: Press releases can also be issued in response to a crisis or negative news. In this situation, a press release can help to provide accurate information and clarify any misinformation that may be circulating in the media.

It is also important to consider the timing of a press release. Issuing a press release at the right time can help to maximize media coverage and generate interest. For example, if a press release is issued during a slow news cycle, it is more likely to receive coverage than if it is issued during a busy news cycle when there are many competing stories.

In conclusion, knowing when to issue a press release is a critical skill for media relations professionals. Press releases should only be issued when there is significant news to share, and the timing should be carefully considered to maximize media coverage and generate interest. By understanding the timing of press releases, media relations professionals can help their organizations or clients achieve their media relations goals and reach their target audiences.

- What is a media advisory, and how can one draft it?

A media advisory is a concise document designed to notify journalists and editors of upcoming events or opportunities for news coverage. This type of communication is typically sent to targeted media outlets and journalists who are likely to be interested in the event, announcement, or story being promoted. A media advisory is not the same as a press release, which is a more detailed document that provides additional background information and quotes. Instead, a media advisory is a brief, straightforward notification that captures the most essential information and encourages journalists to attend the event or follow up for further details.

The structure of a media advisory is relatively simple, and it typically includes the following elements:

1. Heading: The heading should clearly indicate that the document is a media advisory and provide a brief summary of the event or opportunity being promoted.
2. Event Information: This section should include the date, time, and location of the event, as well as any other relevant logistical details, such as parking instructions or special access requirements.
3. Key Messages: In this section, the most critical points of the event should be highlighted, such as the purpose of the event or announcement, the main speakers or participants, and the potential impact or significance of the news being shared.
4. Contact Information: This section should provide the name, title, phone number, and email address of the media contact who can provide additional information or arrange interviews with key spokespeople.

When drafting a media advisory, it is essential to keep in mind that journalists are typically bombarded with dozens or even hundreds of pitches each day. To stand out from the crowd, a media advisory must be concise, compelling, and tailored to the interests and needs of the targeted media outlets and journalists. Some tips for crafting an effective media advisory include:

1. Be clear and concise: A media advisory should be no more than one or two pages, and the language should be straightforward and easy to understand. Avoid jargon, technical terms, or overly complicated language that may confuse or bore the reader.

2. Be timely: The media advisory should be sent well in advance of the event or announcement to allow journalists enough time to plan their coverage. Ideally, the media advisory should be sent at least a week before the event, and follow-up reminders should be sent a few days before and the day of the event.

3. Be targeted: The media advisory should be sent only to media outlets and journalists who are likely to be interested in the event or

announcement. This requires research and knowledge of the media landscape and the preferences and interests of individual journalists.
4. Be strategic: The media advisory should be part of a broader media relations strategy that includes other tactics, such as press releases, media pitches, and social media outreach. A well-coordinated media relations campaign can generate broader coverage and more significant impact than a single media advisory.

For example, a media advisory could be used to promote the launch of a new product or service. The media advisory might include the date, time, and location of the launch event, as well as a brief description of the product or service and its potential benefits to customers. The advisory might also highlight the key spokespeople or executives who will be present at the event and provide a contact name and number for journalists to arrange interviews or request additional information. By crafting a compelling media advisory and targeting it to the appropriate media outlets and journalists, a media relations professional can generate interest and coverage for the launch event and raise awareness of the new product or service.

In summary, a media advisory is a critical tool in a media relations professional's toolkit. It is a concise and effective way to notify journalists and editors of upcoming events or opportunities for news coverage. By following the best practices outlined above and tailoring the media advisory to the interests and needs of the targeted media outlets and journalists, media relations professionals can generate interest.

- What is a media pitch, and how can one develop it?

A media pitch is a persuasive communication that aims to capture the attention of a journalist or editor and encourage them to cover a story. The ultimate goal of a media pitch is to secure positive media coverage for a client, organization, or brand. As a media relations professional, it is crucial to have a solid understanding of what a media pitch is, how to develop one effectively, and how to tailor it to specific media outlets.

Crafting a successful media pitch begins with identifying a newsworthy angle or story that is relevant to the target audience of the media outlet being pitched. A newsworthy angle could be a product launch, a new study or survey, a major announcement, or an event. Once you have identified the angle, it is essential to craft a pitch that is clear, concise, and attention-grabbing.

The first step in developing a media pitch is to research the media outlet and its audience. It is important to understand the tone and style of the media outlet, as well as its focus and areas of interest. This information can be gathered by reviewing past articles or segments and identifying patterns or themes. Additionally, understanding the audience of the media outlet can help to identify what types of stories or topics they are most interested in.

After researching the media outlet and its audience, the next step is to develop a compelling headline or subject line. The headline or subject line should be attention-grabbing and succinct, while also accurately conveying the story or angle being pitched. It should also be tailored to the tone and style of the media outlet being pitched. For example, a headline for a business publication might be more formal and straightforward, while a headline for a lifestyle publication might be more creative and playful.

Once you have crafted an attention-grabbing headline or subject line, the next step is to develop a concise and compelling pitch. The pitch should provide context and detail about the story or angle being pitched, while also highlighting why it is newsworthy and relevant to the media outlet's audience. It should also be tailored to the tone and style of the media outlet, using language and references that resonate with their readers or viewers. It is important to keep in mind that journalists and editors receive numerous pitches every day, so it is crucial to make the pitch stand out and pique their interest.

In addition to crafting a strong pitch, it is important to follow up with the journalist or editor after sending the pitch. Following up can help to reinforce the importance of the story and keep it top of mind. However, it is important to be respectful of the journalist or editor's time and not be too pushy or aggressive.

It is also important to remember that not all pitches will be successful. Some pitches may not resonate with the journalist or editor, or they may not have the capacity to cover the story at the time. It is important to remain professional and respectful, even if the pitch is not successful. Building a positive relationship with journalists and editors can increase the chances of future pitches being successful.

Overall, developing a successful media pitch requires careful research, thoughtful crafting, and a strong understanding of the media outlet and its audience. By following these steps and remaining persistent, media relations professionals can increase the chances of securing positive media coverage for their clients or organizations.

- What are the recommended practices for presenting to journalists?

As a media relations professional, presenting to journalists is a crucial aspect of our job. The way we present our story or pitch can make the difference between getting coverage or being ignored. Below are some recommended practices for presenting to journalists that can increase the chances of getting our story or pitch picked up.

1. Research the journalist and their media outlet

Before reaching out to a journalist, it is important to do some research about them and their media outlet. This includes understanding their beat or area of coverage, the type of stories they usually cover, their audience, and their editorial style. By understanding these factors, we can tailor our pitch to the journalist's interests and increase the chances of getting our story picked up.

For example, if we are pitching a story about a new healthcare technology, we may want to research journalists who cover healthcare, technology, or science. We can also look at the media outlet's past coverage to get a sense of their editorial style and the type of stories they usually cover.

1. Craft a compelling and concise pitch

Journalists receive numerous pitches every day, so it is important to make our pitch stand out. We should craft a pitch that is compelling, concise, and tailored to the journalist's interests.

A compelling pitch should highlight the most interesting and newsworthy aspects of our story. We should also avoid using jargon or technical terms that may confuse or bore the journalist. Instead, we should use language that is clear and easy to understand.

A concise pitch should be no longer than a few paragraphs or a minute-long elevator pitch.

Journalists are busy and don't have time to read lengthy pitches or listen to lengthy explanations. By keeping our pitch concise, we can make it easier for the journalist to digest and consider.

1. Use a personalized and respectful approach

When reaching out to a journalist, we should use a personalized and respectful approach. This includes addressing the journalist by name, using a polite tone, and avoiding aggressive or pushy language.

We should also respect the journalist's time and deadlines. If a journalist is not interested in our pitch, we should thank them for their consideration and move on. We should also avoid bombarding them with multiple follow-up emails or phone calls, as this can be perceived as annoying or harassing.

1. Provide relevant and reliable information

When presenting to journalists, it is important to provide relevant and reliable information. This includes supporting our pitch with data, research, or expert opinions. We should also make sure that our information is accurate and up-to-date.

Providing relevant and reliable information not only strengthens our pitch, but also helps establish our credibility as a source. Journalists are always looking for trustworthy sources, so by providing accurate and useful information, we can build a long-term relationship with the journalist and increase the chances of getting future coverage.

1. Be prepared for questions and follow-up

After presenting our pitch to a journalist, it is important to be prepared for questions and follow-up. Journalists may have additional questions or need more information before deciding to cover our story. We should be ready to answer their questions promptly and professionally.

We should also be prepared to follow up with the journalist if we don't hear back from them within a reasonable time frame. Following up can help remind the journalist of our pitch and increase the chances of getting coverage.

In conclusion, presenting to journalists is a key aspect of media relations. By researching the journalist and their media outlet, crafting a compelling and concise pitch, using a personalized and respectful approach, providing relevant and reliable information, and being prepared for questions and follow-up, we can increase the chances of getting our story or pitch picked up. Remember, the goal is not just to get coverage, but also to build long-term relationships with journalists that can benefit us and our clients in the future.

- What are the ways to establish rapport with journalists and editors?
- What are the essential components of a successful media interview?
- How can one prepare for a media interview?
- What are the recommended steps to take if one is misquoted or their information is inaccurately presented?
- How should one deal with negative publicity or a PR crisis?
- What is an op-ed, and how can it be utilized for media exposure?
- How can one compose a letter to the editor or submit a guest column?
- What is included in a press kit?
- What are the methods for measuring the success of media relations efforts?
- How can social media be utilized to support media relations strategy?

- How can media relations be used to build a personal brand?
- What are some common errors to avoid in media relations?
- How can media coverage be leveraged to expand a small business or advance a career?
- What is media training, and is it a worthwhile investment?
- What are some ways to make one's story newsworthy?
- How can one tailor their pitch to different media outlets?
- What tools and resources are available for media relations?
- What is the role of a media relations professional or agency?

About Author

Ashley Wiley-Morris Paretto's commitment to creating a more woman-focused company goes beyond just implementing policies and programs that support women in the workplace. She has worked to ensure that the company's culture is inclusive and supportive of all employees, regardless of gender, race, or ethnicity.

By creating an environment where everyone feels valued and supported, Paretto has increased employee morale, leading to higher levels of job satisfaction and engagement. When employees feel valued, they are more likely to be invested in the company's success and work harder to achieve common goals.

In addition to the positive impact on employee satisfaction and engagement, Paretto's efforts have also led to increased profits for Hype Snagger. Research shows that diverse and inclusive workplaces are more innovative, have better decision-making processes, and are more effective at problem-solving, leading to increased productivity and financial performance.

Overall, Paretto's dedication to creating a more inclusive and supportive workplace has had a significant impact on Hype Snagger's success, both in terms of employee satisfaction and business growth.

Ashley Paretto's Master's degree from Full Sail University has not only allowed her to grow in her role as Chief Strategist at Hype Snagger but also make it a more woman-focused company. Her dedication to creating opportunities for women in the workplace has made a significant impact, and it is clear that her future is bright.

www.ingramcontent.com/pod-product-compliance
Lightning Source LLC
Chambersburg PA
CBHW031534210526
45464CB00013B/1261